Fade into Obscurity

Scott Shaw

BUDDHA ROSE PUBLICATIONS

First Edition 2016

ISBN 10: 1-877792-93-4
ISBN 13: 978-1-877792-93-9

Library of Congress Control Number: 2016960053

10 9 8 7 6 5 4 3 2 1

Printed in the United States of America

fade in:

girl
skateboarding
down the sidewalk
parallel
to the beach
next
to the water

she sings loudly
out of tune
feet/legs
extend/propels/compels
her movement forward
to somewhere/to nowhere

again
again
again
she kicks
sole to the pavement
       wheels scraping along the ground
       she continues to sing
       loudly
       out of tune
          is this pavement soul?

eventually
she fades into the distance
her voice fades
the sound of her wheels fade
then
she is gone

gone
gone
gone beyond

gone just like the mantra
gone forever

this girl
barista
by trade
sassy
by nature
      sometimes those things
      are so obvious
she has this arrow
tattooed on the inside of her forearm
      that's it
      nothing more
      no further ink
      just an arrow

me, I stand in line
awaiting my turn to order
order from her/the barista
that girl there
      behind the cash register

she… she takes the orders of the others
but her eyes
they continually find their way to me

     …this could be interesting…

finally
my turn has come
me, I approach
she, she asks me
what do I want
I tell her
then, I question
where's that arrow pointing?

she smiles
she answers
right now it is pointing at you

sometimes people stare at me
    ...they know who I am

sometime people
lock their vision

what they think/what they are thinking
I know not

sometimes people
try to take photos of me
on the sly
    I don't like that
if they asked
it would be no problem
but they do not ask
    if I see them
        in the action
    I cover my face

sometime people
notice me

sometime I notice them
noticing me
    if they didn't look so hard
    if the didn't stare so long
    then/they/that moment
    would just pass by
    without a thought
    lost
    to the images
    lost
    to the hands of god

lost
to the moment(s) in time

sometimes people
see me
me, I see them
seeing me
they stare/so I stare
stare
through the protection
of my dark sun glasses
      the glass
      keeps me
      shielded
      my eyes
      hiding
      behind them

      they
      the dark sun glasses
      offers me
      a realm of protection
      from those who see me
      when I don't want to be seen

sittin' in the distance
a glass of wine in my hand
the reaming rays of the sun
etch the sky with a red vibrancy
white clouds
shield the ocean from my eyes

my mind wanders
lost to the distance of the distance
but then it is brought back to my attention
to the attention of others

I hear a woman screaming in pleasure
a man exclaiming his approval
I hear
heavy breathing in the distance
it/this/they
it goes on for a time
          a short time
then it is gone
silence returns
the sound(s) of sex is over

me, I smile
me, I take another drink from my glass
the glass, that occupies my hand
me, I stare back off into the distance
to the red etching the sky
          my mind again wanders

have you ever sat across the table from someone
while
your heart/your soul/your brain
is pounding with a hangover
and they/them/those have no idea
why you feel the way you do

have you ever been with someone
who walks the straight and narrow
while you have drifted
drifted into the realms of the obscure for so long
that you no longer even understand
what the straight and the narrow is

have you ever lived
so far on the outside
lived it for so long
that all you know
is all you know
and everything else is so abstract
lost in the realms of realism
that you have no desire
to re-enter
whatever it is
that was long ago forgotten

have you ever spent
long nights
lost with you and the bottle
while your woman
finds her way
lost to the solitude of the sheets
… this
while you asked her to dance

… this
while you asked her to play
this…
but she could never understand
the rules of the game

have you ever written your poetry
in the dark
because all that is
is all that was
and you are cursed
by the ways of the world

I could tell you that this is me
but you already know that
…cursed
…damned
…cast to the realms of the
        whatever that/this is
        of whatever all artists have screamed about
… this
while others
dance in the light
dance in the day
have hope for tomorrow
of which
I have none

so I sit here
at these computer tying keys
scribble
the realization(s)
of this drunken mind

and dream that it was all different
that it was all whole
that all that dreams
had equaled more than simply
living the drunken vision
of a drunken mind
lost
as I hope
that in the AM
I will not simply wake up
to another killer hangover
that no one else
will understand

welcome
to the realm
of the have-not
dreamer(s)

good girl face
good girl words
good girl clothing
she even has a bit of a tear
in her eyes

but
when she runs her fingers
along my back
gently moving them
from side-to-side
you can tell
there is a demon
inside of her

the question
        do I dance
        do I leave
        do I fall within this demon's grasp
        or do I turn and run away

seven

I'm sloshed/altered
3:35 AM
I wake up
after sleeping for an hour or two

I do this all the time

wake to the:
       semi-sick
       semi-hung-over
       semi-wondering-why

why… do I do this
day after day/night after night

but the allure of the drink
the wine/the women
the promise of the abstract
the hoping for…
the breaking thought the illusion
       it holds its grasp upon me
       it has a tight hold

so, I get up
leave the bed
leave the bedroom
I hit the fridge
I get a drink of water
I walk to window
I open the shades
I stare out into the night-ness
I gaze out over the black sea
in the distance

tonight
I see no moon on the horizon
so I see no light
      glistening upon the water

there is nothing
only blackness
only the knowing/the hoping
that it is still there
this/that/the ocean
when there is nothing to see

with no distant illusion
to hold my mind transfixed
I close the blinds
I turn
I walk in the direction of my bedroom
      a lady lay in my bed
      me, I am:
            semi-sick
            semi-hung-over
            semi-wondering-why
            but I am not alone
I guess this will have to do
I go back to a restless sleep

people get old
people change
me too
me too

I remember reading this review
about Bukowski
it stated how he had lost it
       how now
       he writes about cats
       how whatever revolution
       he had created
       happened back in
           the 60s/the 70s
       but then it was gone
       he was past his prime

but what does a person/a poet
have to write about:
pussy and fucking forever?
why can't they move on?

it is just like life
people want to hold you
hold you
       to what/where you once were

but when you are no longer that
no, not any more
then what?

but life and times
all changes

then
one/we/me/I
is only damned by the memories
of what once was
        what they/me/he/she once were

so me/now
        I am who I am here
                not who I was then
I look to different venues
venues that more conform
to the now that I find myself locked within

sure, I miss the past
sure, I wish it were different
sure, I wish I was young again

but what choice do I have?
what choice do any of us have?
        we get old
        and that is that

we change our worlds
we change our focus
we remember/we dream
of what once was
but all that is left
is what we are
while all that we were
               is gone

of us
those who write about that/this

of the then
of the what was
all we can do is remember
the then/the what was
we do this
as we talk about that
      our current reality

we can reminisce
other(s) can remember
who we once were
but, this is life
and with each step
each ticking of the clock
we come closer to death

all that we were
is left only to memory
all that we are
is a shadow of our former self

so you can write/you can talk about
who was what, when
but you are not them
you are only you
and just like everyone else
you too are getting older
      get ready for it
      here it comes
      live with it
      then die

thorn bush
in the planter
strapped to a fence
dead
it looks very dead
but its thorns
they survive
they still remain

death
in the making
danger
for the taking

this is like life
life
after death

all that remains
is the danger

a day
w/ nothing to do
a day where
nothing needs to be done

I sit
I drink a latte'
        nonfat, of course
I stare out onto the sea
a helicopter
flies by
tracing the shore

grey
the sky is grey
covered in
hazy/white tinted clouds

the ocean
it is grey
light traces of varying shades
        of verging shades
it etches its way
across the surface

somewhere
somewhere out there
in the distance
the two meet
        the ocean
        and the sky
me
I sit
hypnotized

a day
with nothing to do
a day
where
nothing needs doing

I drink a latte'
            nonfat, of course
and I allow my mind to wander
to become lost
in the suchness
of the nothing
            perfect zen

eleven

I was being driven
driven, though the countryside
in southern china
    it was sunny
    the day was warm
the coast approaches
and there in the distance
rising from the ashes
    the ashes
    that were
    and are to come
nuclear resonance
a power plant
waiting to explode
    its colors:
        grey
        blue
        dark/distant
    like a pathway to the heavens
        a roadway
    that no one wants to take

the road proceeds
ahead of us
we drive
down its form-fitted path
the afternoon
is upon us

we drive
    to the left
a house/a structure
three women outside

one stands
in what can only be described
as a parking lot
        a dirty-dirt parking lot

a dirty-dirt parking lot
in front of a dirty house

red lipstick
bright/gaudy
it permeates the air
        the expansive art of space

I look
my driver looks
she sees me
I see her
        she waves
        screams
        wants me to come over
my driver looks to me
checking on my desire(s)

thought the thought did cross my mind
for this sweet young woman of the street
me, I did decline

most men/most women
look to the one that got away
        the person they loved
        but never had

me, I have none of those

none that I cared about
yet, did not know

instead
me, I have her
that hooker/red lipstick
etched in the sky in china
      every now and then
     I think of her
         think
I should have hit it
just to say I did it
but, I did not

just another lost memory
in/of a lost life

thinking of china
I think back then
to one of those
back whens…

I think to a girl I loved there
I just re-read a book of poems
I wrote about her/us
      back then/back when

here/now
I think to the woman
my L.A. lady that I came back to
      back then/back when
after shanghai

when…
when all of it
all we were
her and I
I and china
I and that shanghai girl
had lived
until there was no more living to do
done
so I hit back
back L.A. way
I and L.A.
I and my
L.A lady

but the fact is/was
done/gone/over

it was gone (she and me) long before I left
before I left to live my life
in the dark/deadly arms of china

but I pretended it wasn't that way
        pretended to her/there
        pretended to her/then
                gone/over/done
but you always need someone
to come back to
set your life up that way
if you don't
then/when
whatever what was
        isn't any more
when you come back/home
the alone can kill you

I never told her
her, my L.A. lady
        (my L.A. lady of then)
what I had done
who/what I had hung with
she
as always
was simply
patiently awaited my every return
return to her arms
return to her love

but, me
that time
I came back different

different than any time before
different from life
different from who I was when

came to/came back to that needed utility someone
that someone who need me
someone who mattered no more
though I never told her the truth

but I think back to you
you, my L.A. lady (of then)
of when/way back when
I think how you never knew
I think it was probably better that way
        long gone
        long lost
        long dead
        one of my women
        my woman of shanghai

        long gone
        long lost
        not dead
        at least I don't think so…
        my L.A. lady
        of way back when

but that's just life
we live
and we keep most of it a secret
a secret
a secret for/from
those who should never know

a life lived
that no one will ever know about
that's how you know
you have really lived

long gone
long lost
long dead
something that each of us will be
someday…

silence is golden

how may times
do I drink
drink too much
so I can forget
drink so much
so I can't remember

how many times do I drink
drink so I will wake up
hung over
so I don't want to do anything
so I have a reason
to do nothing

drink
so I will be
way too sick
to drink the next day/the next night
drink…

and this is the life
the life that everyone dreams of
the life of the arts
art
to no one's ears/no one's eyes
but
is it art
none-the-less

me, I don't know…
but me, I know the drink
so that is what I do
I do and I do and I do

do
do, till there is no tomorrow

this is my life
welcome to it
an illusion/a dream
a hope with no meaning

this is art

fourteen

driving by
there's a young girl sitting
sitting, crossed legged, in a street park
her hair
long and blonde
parted down the middle
she wears jeans
a tie-dyed tee shirt
has a cigarette in her hand
      she smokes as the cars pass by

my mind flashes
      is this 1968?
      no
      this is 2014
but there she sits
straight out of the straight out of…

      view
      a glimpse into the past
      the past repeating itself

it all sends me to dreaming
dreaming of the then
dreaming of the what once was
but is no more
dreaming of the how it used to be
      freedom/love
      was in the air
now, there is nothing
nothing to dream for
just a pretty girl sitting in a park
reminding me of what once was

sitting outside one of the coffee-houses
I attended
it is a cool/cloudy afternoon
      the smell of danger and fear
      is in the air

me, I sit drinking a cup of the dark mud
staring off into the realms
where there is no forgiveness

one of the coffee-cookers comes out/comes up
she takes a seat at my table
she smiles
she tries to make small talk
      …I hate small talk

she is old/white/chubby
the grey roots of her dyed hair
flash their way through the
      blonde dye-job

she looks at me
she puts her hand atop mine
she says,
      you know
      I would give you anything
        you want
I look at her
      my answer
but I don't want anything from you

waiting for the rain

the clouds grow in the sky
the so. cal. palm trees blow in the wind
      higher
      above the heads of us all
the warm air is cooling
and the movement of this moment
is cast to this only written memory
      for all else/from everyone else
      it will be lost/forgotten
          never remembered
      but for me/us
      you/me
      here it is
      cast
      to time immemorial

sitting here
a cup in front of me
      outside
      the sound of the city pounding
          as I/we
          you/me
          wait for the rain

there is this asian woman
who lives in this apartment behind me

she is rolie-polie
her rice belly in large and round
somehow this adds to her allure, however
      why
      I do not know

she has the traditional small asian boobs
      clean shaven
      on the
      down there/down below/down low

at night
once the sun goes down
I often sit on my patio
a glass of grape in my hand
I watch the sun set into the sea
but she
there she is
she calls my attention
to her
she never closes the blinds
      of her bedroom window
she struts
there for the world/there for me to see

she comes out of the shower
      dries herself off
            standing there
            full-frontal
I often wonder
does she do it just for me

or does she do it
for the world to see

maybe
       I will never know

now
when her nighttime light is on
I look out my window
I look out to see
I call her my *peep-show*
my peep-show princess
what will she have
to show me tonight

eighteen

a sunny warn early march day
out at the beach
      this winter
      has been unjustly hot

a barefoot girl
skateboards by
      she stops
      pulls out her smartphone
      takes a photograph of the ocean
      sends it to/posts it to
      someone/something/somewhere
she puts her phone back in her pocket
skateboards off

an old man walks by
pushing his wheeled walker
wearing a hat
to protect his aged skin from the sun
      he
      unlike the skateboard girl
      moves his wheels along
         very slowly

a couple walks by
they reek of weed
      out here
      in the outside
      and it can still be smelled
         they must have smoked a lot
this makes me smile
      high at the ocean
         high on the shoreline
            high…

a woman pulls up in her black SUV
UCLA alumni
it says so around her license plate
    she gets out
    east indian of origin
    she helps her daughter out
        maybe two/maybe three
        in full-on jain attire

she stands near me
a camera in one hand
her daughter in the other
    she poses her little girl
    takes photos of her
    the ocean as a backdrop

the sun
the ocean
the warm air
me/like them
them/the other people
here/like me
lost
lost in the lost
    time
    in the ticking
    feeling/knowing
    this is the only thing I ever cared about
    the essence of the ocean

black man
standing in the checkout line
    new ink
    on his very old neck

    how old are you
asks the lady in front of me
    eight-six
    he answers

my first though
    he looks pretty good for eighty-six

he pays
she pays
I pay
    outside
    I see him
two canes
    I think that should be his name
two canes

two canes
the kind with four little padded feet
the kind to keep the person
using them
    up-right/up-straight
he has one in each hand

I look
I watch
I see
    one step/two steps/three

steps
maybe one inch at a time
　　　going nowhere
　　　so fast it is slow

I question
how does he get anywhere
it must take him a week
to walk a block

one step
two steps
three
　　　walking
　　　but going nowhere
two canes
one in each hand

　　　this is what it is to be
　　　eighty-six
　　　with new ink on your neck

white girls in hollywood, 2015
    blonde hair
    brown hair
    they dress 1985
    they dress 1992
    but they don't dress 2015
what does 2015 dress like anyway?

back then/back there
there was a style
now, not so much

white girls in hollywood, 2015
they walk the streets
go into the shops
searching/seeking
what are they looking for

all I see is dirty/danger
maybe they see something else
maybe they seek the dream
    the dream of what
      I have always questioned
    the dream of who
    remains in my mind

white girls in hollywood, 2015
they are here for some reason
    here
but obviously not from here
    but here
    is gone
    as here
    is nowhere

deep
long lost memory
a girl's face
      her body
they come to my mind

young
we were young then
younger
way-way younger than now

then…
then there was purpose
then…
then there was promise
then…
then there was possibility
then…
then there was still the chance
      the chance to make it last
          make life
          something more
but me
me, I walked away
why
I do not really know
I do it all the time

me
me, I left
      left the we
for better promises
on the horizon I suppose

her image
it popped into my mind
as I lay here
deep/deeply into life
        so much of it gone

her image
her face
her body
her sex
I remember them all
what I cannot remember
is her name

insane guy
sitting outside
of the starbucks
        nuts
        shit raving insane

he speaks
yells to the wind
in some strange language
that only he can understand

he cries out
to allah
he screams
amen
he drinks
his frappuccino
he eats
his starbucks oatmeal

life
insanity
ambience
in a city of sin
a city of life
a city of insanity

I suppose
like all of us
he is just living
his own vision
of disenchanted reality

I suppose
he is just doing it
much more loudly
than the rest of us
but we are all the same

the cops pull up
the cops talk to him
the cops do not arrest him
he finishes his frappuccino
he grabs his dirty bag
he slings it across his dirty jacket
over his dirty shoulder
        he walks away

the cops watch him
as he leaves/as he walks down the street
in the direction of the beach

they watch/they listen
nothing said/nothing more spoken
he has move his inanity
to somewhere else

one minute
early
two minutes
late
defined by our circumstance
hindered by life

and is there ever a way out
any-way to find a way in
can we ever have what we really want
or is our reality
simply defined by the desire(s) of others

can we have
w/out the need to give
can we win
w/out the necessity to lose

win/lose
stay/draw
      a chance
      a moment
      defined by all of those
      around us

please, give me a new life

wasted world
wasted day
wanted a different way

way
this way
way
not that way
way…

and I wish it were different

big
fake dreadlocks
big
fake boobs
      chocolate lady
tight
turquoise skirt
tight
black top

her/she
exhibits
who she is/what she is/how she is

not what she could be
for she already is
      the all/the everything

there
complete
paid for

a price worth paying?
but what is the cost?

across the street
I see them
standing there
waiting for the light to change
       they hug
       they kiss
yes
       right there
       on the street
total emersion
in the juices of love

the light changes
they walk across the street
       moving my direction

they come
they arrive
sit down
across from me
at a restaurant by the sea
       the waves crash
       over there
       to my right
       over there
       in the distance
           sea blue/sky grey
they
the sea and the sky
merge
into the nothing of nothing
but this
this is here
this is something

the couple
they have sat
they gaze
into each other's eyes
them
the man/the woman
lost in the juices of love

then, he speaks
she does not
his voice
verging on the loud
I cannot help but listen
listen…
he/she

he tells her how
she has messed up his life
she is messing with who he is
tells her
how she is holding him back

        love lost in the distance
        love seen in the distance
        love there
        is not love here
            seen there
            but not witnessed here

love
like all of life
        an illusion
        a thought

a want
a dream
a desire
we are told
that it is what we should have
what we must have
what we should strive for

but across the street
is never the love
that is sitting down

all an illusion
all a lie

love lived/love lost
defined by the factions of he reactions
        like life…
it means nothing
it is only in the mind

twenty-seven

the warm desert air
blows across L.A.

I can't say that I like it
but it is what it is

here I am
there it is
      the wind and me
lost w/in each other's touch

lost
blowing to no-where

and where does the wind go anyway?
      lost
      like life

      you live
      you feel
      then, like the wind
      you are gone

twenty-eight

I remember this lightening storm
in tibet
etched in abstract colors
connecting the aurora borealis
      sky to earth

earth
tibet
a million miles above the rest
but a million miles none-the-less

earth/sky
sky/earth
electricity

night
colors
etches upon the canvas
the canvas of life
I was there/then
then is what I remember

lightening strikes
off in the distance
transporting the gods to the ground

twenty-nine

this actress contacted me on facebook
asked me
       when was I doing my next film
told me
       she would love to be in it

I looked her up
I looked back when
then…
…she was stunning
       beautiful
               then
          in the1970s
now
2015
she is old
deep in her sixties
old
looking for a new gig
a job
in one of my films

then
       yes
now
       why

I can only think
       I wish I knew her then
life
       it is a sad process

old is old
       old is ugly

in it is a warm/not hot
september night
along the so. cal coastline

I sit on my couch
I look out/across my patio
I see the lights of malibu
off in the far distance
       far/distance
       so. cal.
       coastline

I get up off of my couch
as usual
a glass of the evening grape
it is in my hand
       a bottle/no two
       downed
there is nothing to lose
no-where to go
no/no-thing

all there is, is this
a warm/not hot
september night
       the grape
       a glass
       a bottle/no two
       downed
lost to my thought(s)
as I sit
       look out
       to the sea
           across the sea

thinking this/this life
should have been/should be
something more

I stand up/go out
          out onto my patio
see the sea/closer to the sea
I stand in the evening air
          hot/dead/no life
                    in the heat
                    there is never life

I stand there
stand there in the september heat
a glass of the grape in my hand
the dark/nighttime ocean
in front of my eyes
thinking/wishing that this/this life
should have been/should be
something more
but it is not
this is all it is
a warm/not hot
septemeber night
malibu off there in the distance
a bottle of the grape/no two
down
and me
wishing that my life had been something more

thirty-one

I live overlooking the pacific ocean
to my left
      my visual land-form vision
is flanked by santa catalina island
to my right
I see all the way up the coast
      to point mugu
on clear night
      I can see the lights of ventura/camarillo
radiating in the distant sky
over the santa monica mountains

below me
between me and the sea
resides a golf course
sometimes I sit on my patio
and watch
as people take their golf clubs
and their golf balls and try to guide
them into a hole on the putting green
      they practice and practice
      they try and try
      to guide their ball towards their
          desired destination
me
I cannot help but wonder
why
waste your life doing nothing
doing something
that means nothing
pretending that what you are doing
equals anything

a ball
a hole
a golf club
and a person
with nothing better to do
it truly baffles me

thirty-two

I sit out on my patio at night
under the stars
looking out to the black sea
which lays out into infinity
        in front of me
     a glass of the grape in my hand
        of course
periotic lights up the coast
illuminate the illuminati
     of which I am one
the time is soft/easy/complete
     meditative

there exists a parking lot in front of me
there, between me and the sea
     the black sea
it is some distance away
but I see it clearly
     it is for a golf course
     populated only in the day
     sometime
        at the four o'clock AM hour
     I see the workers
     driving their way in
     preparing for the day ahead

     …sometimes
     on those times when I am awake
     at that hour
        coming home
        from the other side
        of midnight

many times
       I see a car stuffed lonely and alone
       in that parking lot
            isolated deep
            in the late night
I wonder what is going on
inside that car
       is somebody getting a blow job
       smokin' some weed
       maybe they're doing the dirty betty
       in the back seat
            I know don't know
            I will never know

last night
I sit on my patio
the stars above me
the black sea in front of me
the distant lights of the illuminati
etching the coastline
       a car drives up
       the only car in the parking lot
       it parks under a parking lot lamp
       stays there a few minutes
       then moves
I think they are leaving
       but no
they just go and park
under a different light
       okay…
but then they do it again
they go back to their original light

why I wonder
                   but no answer comes
stop
start
do it again
then again
shifting
between these two street lights

I tried/attempted
to figure it out
I could not
          it went on and on and on and on
          maybe ten times

me, I could take it no more
I took my glass of wine
went inside
sat on my couch
and watched some tv

you can always tell
when a person's life is hurting
they buy trinkets and charms
they hang religious objects
   from their door
they smile
   when they want to cry
when asked
they say everything is great
   perfect
but it is not

you can always tell
when someone is hurting
the wear crystals and crosses
   jewish stars and om symbols
they hang chimes on their patios
   god, I hate chimes

you can always tell
when someone is hurting
   they seek the answers everywhere
   pray to the gods above
   go to church
   listen to the lies
and do everything but the thing
that will actually help them
   change

driving down the street
listening to the radio
      PCH in the LBC
one of those times when
the music is bumping
      sounding good
      and it looks like
      everyone/everywhere
      is moving to the beat

I drive
I listen
I look
      movin'/groovin'

I watch/I witness
      as the people
      seem to move with the music
but I'm hit with surprise/sadness
      I open my eyes
      and I see

sight one: an old lady
walking in perfect time
      frail/fat/disgusting
      a cane and a dirty dress

sight two: old/ugly white trash woman
      cigarette in one hand
      phone in the other
      up there on a patio
      looking out to the city
      as she turns in perfect time

but where is the pretty
where is the stylish
where are those
who hold the keys to the dreams
      nowhere
      nothing
      not here
      only the old and the ugly
      killing a perfect moment
      in the perfect beat of time

thirty-five

I drink three things:
    water
    coffee
    wine

I look around me
and everybody is drinking everything
    they have cokes, 7ups, dr. peppers
    mountain dews, orange crush,
    organic sodas, flavored waters
    herbal teas

I hear them ordering the weirdest shit
all the time

    variety is the spice of life
        so they say
but me
I drink three things:
    water
    coffee
    wine

it's like an obstacle course
mutters this old man
       with a four prong cane
as he walks past me
       as I sit
       as I drink coffee
       as I eat a bagel
       at an outdoor bagel shop

old
all I could see/all I could hear
was old

it must be hard to be old

to be old and to know you're old
       it must be very-very hard

how does one become old
me, I do not know

some would say I am old
my years certainly would attest
       to that fact

me, I know my years
       know my age
know how the young must see me
       think of me
but I feel so young
       know I am old
       but feel so young

I doubt that the man
strutting with his four prone cane
        feels that way
as he charts his way
                through the obstacle course

me, never thought I would be this old
me, never though I would live this long
        dead
        somewhere over there in asia
        dead
someway/somehow
        but dead
                just the same

but now
        me
I sit here having a coffee
        a coffee and a bagel
                at an outdoor bagel shop
watch
        as they old walk by me
listen
        as they mutter to themselves

me, wondering how to become old
old
when I feel so young

circa 1970s
walking
      long skirt
      long flowing
          waist length
          wavy hair
a dark haired beauty
young
      young
      like I was then
      then, in the 1970s
my age
the age, I would have been
then/not now

girl
I would have fallen in love with her
then/now

the world has turned/returned
so many times since then
then, the 1970s

the world has turned/returned
come full circle
      the girls all have long/flowing
      hair again
yes, some of the guys do too
there they are
looking for a time
      that they are too young to remember

trying to live/thinking
    the dream was better back then
maybe it was
yeah, I think/believe it was

younger/better/more dreams to live
the possibility of more dreams to come

and there she was
walking right in front of me
a reminder of the desires
    lived/left unlived
a girl/young/beautiful
flowing dark hair
I could have loved her then
I could love her now
but (I guess)
too much time has passed
too long
since the 1970s
when I was young, then
    like she is now

all I can do is remember

thirty-eight

waiting
I stand
waiting
for my drink to be brewed
a latte'
non-fat, if you please
there at the counter
          there by the counter
we wait
as the barista cooks our brews

wow, man
are you a lawyer?
you look just like my lawyer
he has gotten me out of so much trouble
he looks just like you
          he dresses just like you
pony tail
tennis shoes
a sport coat
is that a rolex you're wearing?
he has one too

man
forties
scruffy
          too scruffy
                    for the right side of town
greying hair
shorts
a tee-shirt

looks like a stoner
      a stoner who never stopped
      being a stoner
      thus, and therefore
      he needs a lawyer
probably still lives with his parents
who pay for his lawyer
his lawyer who looks like me

people
life
the dream/the want
the want that they want
the need to be
be of something
the something that leads to nothing
      it is the dream
      and the holders of the dream
      none-the-less

some make something of themselves
some make nothing of themselves
but in truth
what is the difference
we all stand there
waiting for our drinks to be made
made by a barista
      it arrives
      then we are gone
      just like life

a girl looks my direction
she kisses me with her eyes
a stolen glace
that equals an eternity
of all that should be/could be
but it is not/it is gone
        she walked on
        I walked on
chances are
we will never see each other again

how many times
        has this happened in life
how many glances/chances
that came and then they went away
how many/too many

of all that I have had
of all that I could have had
of all that I did not have
what remains
that glance/that kiss
that promise of illusion

life
I wish it could mean more

sitting in/on the outside
a latte' in my hand
        nothing new here

the sun is down
it just went down
I saw it pass behind the hill
        there/over there
down past the horizon

the lost images of light
still radiate
presuming/pretending
that there is still
nothing left to lose

the youth of the masses
they surround me
me
friday day/turning to friday night
        the local high school has let out
I watch
as they scramble to be cool
to be relevant
to be something/anything
something that they are yet to become
        how many will make it?
they speak
of those who are distant
        they talk behind their backs

they yell
they scream
at their friends

they insult the lessor of them
as they try to climb higher
        higher, on the food chain
but yet
but still
there they remain
lost in their youth
too young to know
what will/what is to come
        ...to come

        life...
where we all exist
where we all do
        what we need to do
need to do
        to get by

so, there they are
lost to the realms of youth
lost to the dream
        of the promise
        of the illusion
        of all that is to come
        of all that could be to come
        of all that will never be
though it is all promised

youth
lost
yelling
crying
being

who they try to be
when life is just a projection
of the *never-never*
of the all and the nothing
of the hopes and the dreams

do you remember your youth?
did you become?
or, did you die
at the hands of fate?

forty-one

I used to stay up all night
I would drink wine
and write
and drive the streets of L.A.
looking for some new illusion

3:00 AM/4:00 AM
sometimes I would hit
over to this 24/7 restaurant
in Gardena

how I found it/why I started going there
I don't really remember
but I did and I did

there was this sweet young-ish
japanese/american girl
who used to man the counter
in those late night/early day hours
man it/in all her womanhood

she did something to me
something deep
called out all those
unfulfilled desires

      unfilled desires
      of a lost man
      lost, in the lost night

maybe it was on tuesdays
maybe wednesdays
      I don't really remember

but I would go there
go there and get my late night eats on

go there
talk to her
and dream of the dream
of the dream we could make together
if only we would/could get together

get together?
no, we never did
but that dream did dream on
for a time anyway…

did she have the same dream?
I guess I will never know

but life changed/I changed
I started to do other things
I found other women
to lay my fantasies upon

she
gone
where to
I guess I will never know
that late night dream
of an unfulfilled fantasy
        the longer you live life
        the more you will have

today
by accident

I pulled into that parking lot
the parking lot of that 24/7 restaurant
that I have not been to in so-so many years

I pulled in there
as there is a shopping center behind it
I pulled in there
and I pulled into a parking space
and all of a sudden
I remembered
a parking space I had parked in before
before…
in so many of those late night jaunts
attempting to live the dream
of my lost fantasy

so there I was
thirty years too late/maybe more
same parking spot
restaurant still there
24/7
the girl
long gone, I imagine
me, lost to age

but I still remember her
and I still dream

the night is closing in
it's june
so the timeframe is late
late in the day
late in life

me, I like the winter
the days are short
the temperature is cool
and there is mysticism in the air

the night is closing in
I sit back on my patio
a glass bottle of the brew in my hand

the ocean
it stretches out in front of me
long/lost
grey/blue

the june clouds
have the sun hidden
hidden
out there on the horizon

they are there
the sun is behind them
but its essence
is poking through
      red/orange
      purging the grey/blue

but
there is a space

a space between the clouds and the sea
I am waiting for the sun to emerge
reveal itself
between them and it

and there
if only for a moment
the sun will be the sun
the sky will be the sky
the clouds will be the clouds
and the sea will be the sea

then, if only for a moment…

like life/here then gone
we live only for an instant

sun
darkness
clouds
sea
life
death
and then
like when the sun crests/then set
there is nothing

shop girl
latina
50/100 lbs overweight
could she be pretty
      if she dropped some pounds?
maybe…

you know how it is
somewhere underneath the underneath
somewhere lost deep down inside
some of them
      hidden by the poundage
they are hiding pretty
      is she?
      I don't know?

she looks at me
with eyes of want
do I want her?
maybe…
there is a fantasy there
I can feel it

latina
somehow
they are just so sexy
they get my blood *flown'*

she gives me
that smile
she gives me
that maybe

me, I'm maybe too
      maybe
maybe
      as the years drift on

years drift on
and the availability diminishes
      the what is available
            the what is offered up
      the what I can choose from
            the what I can have

back then
younger days/younger years
I was picky
wanted only the *crème of the crop*
      the best of the best
but the best of then
      they are long gone
they too have gotten old

now
the offers that are offering
are fewer and farther between
they are still there
by the there is this
an overweight latina
with lust in her eyes

the clouds have blown in along the coast
the marine layer is deep
eyesight/foresight is limited
only a few feet
in any direction

that's okay
I have seen enough

in the clouds/in the distance
I hear laughter
people laughing about something

laughter in the distance
laughter in the clouds
laughter in the life
unknown
        no reason why
the perfect form of happiness
as there never is a seeable reason
        of and/or for
                anything

the night rains down hard in bangkok
monsoon/summer
      normally
      it rains only during the day

the etching of the blue/black night touches
      the edging of a skyscraper
            off in the distance

no, this isn't as it used to be
no, this isn't as I wish it still was
but this it
this is all that is left
this is all that I have left
a night
lost in/to the pagan extremes
a night that wishes to be remembered
remembered, a different way
a night
      like so many before
where I never found
what I didn't find
only left with a handful of has-been
poetry
dreaming that it was/like I was
thirty years ago
when I first hit these dirty streets

back then
      when the lie meant something
back then
      when I could have been something

not now
too late
        to late to lie

the night rains/the heat pours
I think back to the loves
that I have known here

loves
they all turned out to be lies
the lies of them
the lies of me
the lies
        all the same

as the rain pours
I think back to that sweet young thing
        a hotel room receptionist

heat
it poured through the hotel
the electricity had shut down
        we spoke
        we talked
she said that no one loved her
I told her I would

a day
a dream
a kiss a night
our lips met

she said she had never

hardened by the lies
I did not believe her
but
she spoke the truth
rip/tear
blood everywhere
her first time/not mine

I never forgave myself
never forgave myself
for not believing her

lived, too many lies
lied to, too many time

blood flowing
on my hotel room carpet
nothing that I could do but
nothing

I think back to her
on these bangkok nights

love lived
love lost
loved lied
I had been lied to
too many times

so here I am
pouring rain

the night heat strangles me
it forces me to remember
if forces me to rethink
it forces me to wonder about
the wondering why

it forces me…

the night rains down hard in bangkok
monsoon/summer
      normally
      it rains only during the day

the etching of the blue/black night touches
      the edging of a skyscraper
          off in the distance

no, this isn't as it used to be

every morning
I look out to the ocean
I study her waves
look to her essence for guidance

some days
the marine layer has cast
      a cloud-filled veil of exclusion
leaving
no ocean to be see

those days are few, however
few and far between
most days
      through the distance
the ocean is always seen
      witnessed

everyday I look to her
I look out across her
me, I count the
boats/ships/barges/vessels
      small or large
      there they be
      out there
      on the sea
I wonder what they are doing
      the people out there
         on them
dancing across the sea

so vast
is she
there you are
so isolated
on her
I think I might be scared

every night
I look out to the sea
I watch the sunset
it all its immersive glory
I study
it etching its way down
across the horizon
orange and red colors
clouds
fixate my mind

I look out to the sea
I count the
boats/ships/barges/vessels
sometimes I see none

none
the perfect essence
no disturbance
nothing
perfect zen

forty-seven

stranded in life
in the middle of hollywood
      hollywood?
      hollywood's just a state of mind

on hollywood b.l.v.d.
my car is having problems
overheating
on this way too hot
june day

june day/hollywood
too hot
I remember it all too well
my days
      youth
      walking these streets
      I used to walk this path
      everyday to high school

junkyard vision(s)
stars on the sidewalk
promises made to the masses
dreams shattered/dreams torn
lives destroyed
      for what?
      for nothing

to me it was always nothing
just a place to live
I never bought into the lie

but years go by/decades, in fact
and here I am again
car having a problem
stuck in the hollywood heat
in the heart of hollywood
hollywood b.l.v.d.
just off of vine street
I've been here/living this
a before I never wanted to live again

hollywood
this must be hell

crenshaw blvd.
early summer 2016
the day is hot
much hotter than normal
too hot—for this time of year
L.A.

>and the *el niño* that was promised
>never came

they've been doing this construction/renovation
on crenshaw

>crenshaw, down here in the hood

new rapid transit

>coming soon/coming through

the street has been a mess
for over a year now
doesn't look like anything
is gong to change any time soon

I see street closure signs

>up ahead

don't want to deal with that

>I hang a right

drive awhile

>then hang a left

north, on the side streets

driving through the run down
a neighborhood in ruins

people of color
sitting outside
      outside cooler than inside
         I surmise

some are old
very little life left
some are younger
I wonder why they have no job
      on the dole, I guess
      free ride
      from a free society

young
black
they sit
the stand
outside
in the heat

outside
trying to look so hard
      prove that they are a thug
      prove that they can sling
      proving what
         not having a job can equal

a pathway to prison
a pathway to destruction
a pathway to proving
that being hard is not that hard

the day is hot
crenshaw is closed
I drive by
north

remembering
that this is not far from where I grew up
        the people
        the same
        thug'n
        proving how hard they are
        but what does that prove
        I do not know

        it only proves a pathway
        to how to waste a life

I turn left
drive a few blocks
I turn right
back on crenshaw again
past the roadwork
past the thugs
past the demise
of the inner city
where hope is so barren
and life holds no promise at all

wake up
look outside
blue sea
in front of me
they day
      summer
warm/not hot
it holds promise
but I wonder
what those promises are

I drive
I open the door
I get out
I go inside
I order
I sit down
I drink a latte'
      non-fat, of course
I ponder my day
as the time ticks on

      what to say
      what to see
      what to do
        and why

but me
I come up with nothing

no idea
      lost
      living
      loving

a perfect day
in an imperfect life
and I have no idea
what to do next

fireworks up the coastline
colored lighted
etched into the blue/black sky

not close enough to hear
but distant enough to see

see across the sea

santa monica
malibu
zuma, I think

distant
but not too distant
not too far to experience this night

remembering back
back thirteen/maybe fourteen years deep
used to live right on the water
redondo beach
the firworks
shot off
off of a barge
a barge just west of the pier
loud lights
etched across the sky—night
so close
too close maybe
it was all too real

now, a decade plus deep
years later/a lifetime later
my lady and I still together

we stood there
this/tonight
she wrapped a blanket around us
cold summer night

we watched/we stared
we looked to the distant sky
colors: red, blue, green, yellow
but if we didn't look
didn't study the distant horizon
nothing would have been seen

the night/this night
it is supposed to mean something
something/I know not what

too lost/too distant/too many years ago
for me to even care
all I know is the me/the her
there we are
in this night
looking to the dark horizon
looking to see

"hey baby, it's the forth of july"

fifty-one

I look out to the sea
in the morning
I always count the ships

I look out to the sea
in the evening
I always count the ships

sometime/tonight
there is none
the sea is empty
only the wave
the ever-flowing ocean current
the essence of life
blue/grey/sometime green
      but rarely that is the case

tonight
grey/blue cloudy sky
etching itself onto the ocean
causing a divining line
where there is no clear definition

clouds to grey/ocean to grey
the colors are perfection/excellence

the night: cool july
almost cold
      that's good
      I like it that way

I sit outside
another glass of the grape in my hand

I watch for the grey fading to black

I look to the sea
try to count the ships
but there are none
         nothing
only me and the sea
the night coming on
a glass of the grape in my hand

if I don't think to hard about it
this could be perfection

warn summer breeze
it blows across
the dense urban landscape
I walk
parallel to the freeway
      a million cars pass by
rush hour
thursday
      everyone
somewhere else better to be

the air
      dry
the sky
      blue/grey/dirty
just like L.A. summers
      always promise

and, yes
there must be someplace better to be
but me
this is all I have

conversation(s)
        talking
it goes on all around me

conversation(s)
        talking
the kind I just don't want to hear

to my right
        urban men
one in shorts
two in causal business attire
one looking for a job
the other two
talking about the ones they already have

SHUT UP!

to my left
        a cop/a black cop
        a black cop
        from the city of el segundo
yes, a black cop in/from
the city if el segundo

for those of you
from a different place/a different time
you will not know
what you do not know
el segundo
early in time/early in space
they would arrest blacks
just for walking their streets at night

arrest them—maybe even in the day

that/then/this
no, it was not that long ago
a generation deep
maybe twenty/thirty years

the tv show
      stanford and son
even made joke about it/that/this
back then
in the 1970s
when that show was on

but I guess
that was a long time ago
      a different time/place
a space
that few of us still remember

but there/here he is
a black cop from el segundo
      talking
talking to white guy
      a white guy and his daughter
also from el segundo
      talking about living in
           el segundo
talking/talking/talking

SHUT UP!

me, I drink my AM starbucks coffee
trying to forget
          …trying to forget…
that I drank too much last night
          drank too much again

I sit outside
a relatively cool summer AM
I sit in/on
the outskirts of el segundo

I sit
listing to people say
          what I have no desire to hear

my brain screams
          there must be a better life

there must be
but I guess not for me

THIS IS LIFE

sometime you meet 'em
sometime you interact with 'em
those young beautiful girls
that show you some interest
they look at you
        just that way
that way you want a girl to look at you

they look at you
and all they see is you
        not the man that is old enough
to be their father/their grandfather

every now and then
you meet 'em
you interact with them 'em
and they set all the desires
        and the dreams
flowing in your mind
        ...all the fantasies
of what could be

what could be in the wishing
        wishing
        that you had something
        to give them
give them something that
they could actually want
        want and lust
        lust and want
                the mind runs circles

they smile at you
that perfect smile

they talk to you
that perfect talk

the mind dreams
lost in the what could be
if you could only be
something
something else
something
other than old

fifty-five

I have this microwave oven
I've had it for a lot of years

it seems microwaves
        last a long time

I've only owned two
        the one before this
        and this one

two in thirty-five
        something like that...

I have this microwave oven
the top of it
        is covered with paint

blue/red/green/yellow
I used to use it for a drying pallet
        a place/space
        where my small paintings
                could dry
I used to
now I don't
but the paint is still there

I guess I could clean it off
but that would be so sad
        as it is art onto itself
art in an artless world

colors swirl
finding their own perfect

            perfection
            in an imperfect world
where only things
mean anything
but things to be
are only what they cannot be seen to be

art
colors
paint
on the top of a microwave over
            one of the two
            the only two
            that I have ever owned

old homeless guy
bum
but you can't really say that anymore
it is politically incorrect
and now
       these days
everything has to be
       politically correct
but he lays there
       lays there
       on the side of the street
his long grey hair
his long grey beard
he's been there for more than a ten years
       a decade deep
he used to lay on this bus bench
burning his face in the sun
       they took his bus bench away
then he laid there
on the patch of astroturf
       the patch of astroturf
       that divided the sidewalk
from where people pump their gas
       yes
       he lay in front of a gas station
       on a busy street
then
somewhere along the way
probably to get him to move along
they put in these three big boulders
       spikey
       jagged
they are not round/they are not soft

but still/now
there he lies
stretched out across the jagged boulders

his eyes are usually closed
as I drive by
       rarely, I see them opened
is he awake/asleep
I know not
but what I do know
is that he is there
that is his spot
his home
laying there
with no better place to be
no where else to go
waiting for his life to begin
or waiting for his life to end

    I often wonder what he is thinking

first-class lounge
three glasses of the grape down
more to come
      pinot noir
          to be exact
two hours till my flight
      flies off
and I am set to dreaming

fifty-eight

the night
it hopes for the illusion
        the promise
                …tokyo
maybe twelve hours off
and I have every dream of the dreamer

beer before wine
      is fine
wine before beer
      always fear

me, I don't know
I always mix my poisons

the feeling/the end result
the only tell

live/die
feel/reveal
pay the price/or no

for life lived without living
what is the point

altered edge
life in the balance
     balance w/out the question of time

all there
all taken away
only a second of a second
it is as it could only be

once was
is

evaporate
into the abyss

but in this moment
I am in this moment
     I live
     life/lived/touched/felt
     give/having
     isn't/is
and then we know/we realize
this is all we have/all we are
     life
     live it

sixty-one

self insolation/annihilation
the drink flows free
as I partake of the elixir

first-class lounge
LAX
the area is empty
        today
only a few flying
the high priced skies

me
I study the bottles
study them
        in the self-serve/serve yourself
                alcohol bar

one bottle
two bottles
three
they are all
                already opened
        no thank you
I don't like
        what has been touched

I check/I find
I crack a new one
        a nice bottle
        of the california grape

a new drink/a new bottle
        mine/only mine

I sit
I drink
I wait
the awaiting
for my plane to be on time
      but it seems they never are

a voice it speaks
sounds, through the loud speakers
spoken in a different tongue
      it will be late
      another hour
      we are sorry
but me
I don't really care
      I have a drink
      I have a bottle
      I have a distance
            out there in the distance
            waiting to be known
            waiting to be lived
summoned
by distant asia
      a time to live
      in a time to come

I wait the awaiting
this is my time
LAX first-class lounge
a bottle next to me
more at the
      self-serve/serve yourself
            alcohol bar

there/over there
      if I need more

me
I sit
I write
I realize
not too bad
as life could be a whole lot worse

sixty-two

here I sit
                dark
…lights out
turned out…

I try to write in the dark

will I be able to read what I have written
        tomorrow

to write
thirty—forty thousand feet
I, in the sky
L.A. to tokyo

lights out
the air hums with the intensity
of jet fueled flight

dark
I could watch a movie from my seat
no
I could listen to music from my seat
no
I could push a button
        and turn my seat into a bed
no

I prefer to write these drunk thoughts
as everyone falls into their dreams around me

dark
live the light

dark
so alluring

dark
so many lies and promises to be had

dark
      to live life
      you have to be awake

sixty-three

latte'
with a heart shaped design
in an italian restaurant
where no one speaks italian

look into the heart
I hate to drink the latte'
it will kill the heart

study the heart
          in the heart of tokyo

my lady
the girl who makes me smile
smiles, as I do not want to drink my latte'

but finally
I look
I think/I drink
the heart touches my lips
kisses my lips

my heart
in tokyo
it was there
but now it is gone

sixty-four

hands clinched
in prayer position
silent words
spoken
a man prays
he crosses himself
then he prays
some more

a church?
no
this is starbucks
       sitting on the patio
       on the bad side of the city

I don't know…
maybe he has a lot to pray for
I don't know…
maybe he has a lot to pray about
so much so that he has to do it in public
while all the others
drink their cups of joe

maybe
I do not know

or maybe
he's just nuts
       yeah, that's it
       probably just a suitable psycho
             uncontained/unrestrained
just sane enough to function
out here in the world

out here
      with us/the sinner
out here
      where there is no god

looking back
girl forgotten
I sit where I sat
so many years ago

I sit
and the memories
smack me/hit me/remind me
I think about
what was
          then/went
so long ago

choices in the wind
choices lost to life
and me, I was the one who made them

girl forgotten
why did she come to mind
distance in the wind
no reason to remember
yet, I remembered
and it did me no good

age-framed
locked in time
little time left

the old/the average
they have made up their minds

minds made up
decisions made/choices lost
they look to the world
with eyes of judgment

fuck them

does anybody like the old?

sixty-seven

early morning
pushing the seven o'clock hour
I'm awake
    awake
from the night before

    why go to bed
    when the new day has dawned

I sit here
stare at this screen
as my fingers
make images/letters appear

this november day
it is cool
the air finds its way in
from the open window in front of me

I look out/I look up
up there
to the AM light blue sky
the moon still rides the horizon
    the moon in the day
    I forever think that is cool

and here it is
this is it
life
    life
    such as life is

I look to the horizon
I look to the sea

I look to the moon that still rides the AM sky
and maybe
>   just maybe
>   this is perfect
>   perfect perfection
>   at least as perfect
>   as I could hope it would be

life lives
I hear the AM birds speaking
talking
somewhere/out there
they live their life
just like me/you
>   here now
>   doing
>   they we will be gone
gone while someone else
see the sights
>   the moon in the AM sky
listens to the sounds
>   the birds
>   saying what they have to say
and feeling life
>   the good/the bad
>   the happy/the sad
feeling
>   when we feel no more

Scott Shaw Books-in-Print include:

About Peace: A 108 Ways to Be At Peace When Things Are Out of Control

Advanced Taekwondo

Apostrophe Zen

Arc Left from Istanbul

Ballet for a Funeral

Bangkok and the Nights of Drunken Stupor

Bangkok: Beyond the Buddha

Bus Ride(s)

Cairo: Before the Aftermath

Cambodian Refugees in Long Beach, California: The Definitive Study

Chi Kung For Beginners

China Deep

Echoes from Hell

Essence: The Zen of Everything

e.q.

Guangzhou: A Photographic Exploration

Hapkido: Articles on Self-Defense: Volume 1

Hapkido: Articles on Self-Defense: Volume 2

Hapkido: Essays on Self-Defense

Hapkido: The Korean Art of Self-Defense

Hong Kong: Out of Focus

Independent Filmmaking: Secrets of the Craft

In the Foreboding Shadows of Holiness

Israel in the Oblique

Junk: The Backstreets of Bangkok

Katmandu and Beyond

Last Will and Testament According to the

Divine Rites of the Drug Cocaine

L.A. Street Shots: A Photographic Exploration

L.A.: Tales from the Suburban Side of Hell

Los Angeles Skidrow: 1983

Marguerite Duras and Charles Bukowski:
           The Yin and Yang of Modern Erotic Literature

Mastering Health: The A to Z of Chi Kung

Nirvana in a Nutshell

One Word Meditations

On the Hard Edge of Hollywood

Pagan, Burma: Shadows of the Stupa

Rangoon and Mandalay

Sake' in a Glass, Sushi with Your Fingers:
Fifteen Minutes in Tokyo

Scream of the Buddha

Scream: Southeast Asia and the Dream

Screenshot Tokyo

Scribbles on the Restroom Wall

Samurai Zen

Sedona: Realm of the Vortex

Shama Baba

Shanghai Whispers Shanghai Screams

Shattered Thoughts

Singaore: Off Center

South Korea in a Blur

Suicide Slowly

Taekwondo Basics

Ten to Thirty

The Chronicles: Zen Ramblings from the Internet

The Ki Process: Korean Secrets for Cultivating Dynamic Energy

The Little Book of Yoga Breathing

The Little Book of Zen Mediation

The Lyrics

The Most Beautiful Woman in Shanghai

The Passionate Kiss of Illusion

The Screenplays

The Tao of Chi

The Tao of Self Defense

The Voodoo Buddha

The Warrior is Silent: Martial Arts and the Spiritual Path

Zen Mind Life Thoughts

The Zen of Life, Lies, and Aberrant Reality

The Zen of Modern Life and the Reality of Reality

TKO: Lost Nights in Tokyo

Urban India: Bombay, Delhi, Lucknow

Varanasi and Bodhi Gaya: Shade of the Bodhi Tree

Wet Dreams and Placid Silence

Woods in the Wind

Yoga: A Spiritual Guidebook

Yosemite: End of the Winter

Zen and Modern Consciousness

Zen Buddhism: The Pathway to Nirvana

Zen Filmmaking

Zen in the Blink of an Eye

Zen Mind Life Thought

Zen O'clock: Time to Be

Zen: Tales from the Journey

Zero One

fade out.

www.ingramcontent.com/pod-product-compliance
Lightning Source LLC
Chambersburg PA
CBHW072126090426
42739CB00012B/3083